OVERLAND ROUTE

TO

INDIA AND CHINA

OVERLAND ROUTE

TO

INDIA AND CHINA

The air of that sweet Indian land,
Whose air is balm; whose ocean spreads
O'er coral rocks and amber beds;
Whose mountains, pregnant by the beam
or the Warm sun, with diamonds teem ;
Whose sandal groves and bowers of spice
Might be a Paradise !

MOORE

ISBN : 978-93-334-4392-0(PB)

First Published, 1859

Published, 2018

Published by

Facsimile Publisher
12 Pragati Market
Ashok Vihar, Ph-2
Delhi-110052
E-mail: books@facsimilepublisher.com

Printed at: G. Print Process, Delhi.

INDEX.

OVERLAND ROUTE

TO

INDIA AND CHINA.

Reader, our voyage is not a short one. If you consent to follow us, we will lead you from under the gray skies of England to those of the golden Mediterranean, where the blue above rivals the blue below; from these we shall advance to the sand-plains of the eastern desert, steam over the waters of the Red Sea and across the glowing waves of the Indian Ocean, to the burning shores of Hindostan. Nay, further, once committed to our care, we will sweep you onward to the isles of the Antipodes, hail the sea-ports of the far east, and rest not until we have cast out our anchor and grappled the distant shores of China!

Art thou ready for such a jaunt? If so, make speedy preparation; and see to it that you give earnest and attentive heed to that invaluable and altogether indispensable "Handbook of Information," published by the "Peninsular and Oriental Steam Navigation Company," whose noble vessel—with flags flying in the breeze and steam up, for the hour of departure has arrived—awaits us at the distance of a gunshot from Southampton Pier. Already her capacious interior has been filled with hundreds of human beings, and thousands of bales and boxes; yet she looks elegant, slender, and *unsatisfied!* But the cargo is complete; the gangway is closed; the command is given; the shrieking steam is checked, and its enormous power allowed to vent itself upon the mysterious engine below, whose deep throb is felt to vibrate gently through the noble ship as we leave the pier behind us; while floating softly from the shore comes the last "hurrah" for the outward bound.

It is as well to state the fact at the outset, that the "Overland Route" to India is performed by *sea*, with the very inconsiderable exception of a little more than 200 miles through Egypt and across the Desert of Suez. No doubt the land portion of the route may be extended, and that of the sea shortened, by journeying through France to Marseilles; but being fond of the sea and not liable to sea-sickness, *we* prefer the voyage to the journey.

And who would not rejoice in the sea—in the free breezes of the great deep—while it receives us on its heaving bosom, and greets us with its fresh breath, as we pass Portsmouth, sweep round the Isle of Wight, and dash down the British Channel? Soon the cliffs of old England grow faint and dim—dimmer to many whose rising tears suffuse their eyes while they gaze wistfully back upon the fading shores of "home." At length the tremulous line vanishes from the most long-sighted vision, and turning, with very different feelings, towards the bow, we look out upon the ocean. Soon we tire of this unchanging view, and now, for the first time, we glance inboard and regard our fellow-passengers. There are upwards of 200 of them, and of these, by far the greater proportion are males, differing as widely in their personal appearance as in their hopes, and fears, and occupations. There are military men—bronzed, quiet, gentlemanly, and grave—returning to the land of their choice, after the usual three years leave of absence. There are civilians—elderly men, mere bones and leather—returning to their adopted country after a vain attempt to exist in their native land, now, alas! too cold to hold them. There are more military men—young, slim, slashing, loud, and addicted to cigars and lisping—who, having the world all before them, have chosen India as a suitable field of glory. These become nautical for the nonce, and line the paddle-boxes after meals, the more conveniently to enjoy the solace of a contemplative smoke. Besides these, there are pleasure-seekers—lovers of travel—men whose circumstances are what is conventionally termed easy, and whose time is at their own disposal. They are good-natured and inquisitive; full of the idea of beholding "the Rock," and enthusiastic about the glories of the Mediterranean; or, in a few cases, imbued with a Mungo-Park-like resolve, to dare the dangers of the desert and explore the secrets of the Nile.

Of the fair sex, there are a few matronly partners of the before-mentioned civilians, and several blooming wives of the before-mentioned grave and bronzed military men; also one or two sickly dames, who are on their way to the genial south in search of health.

Such is the motley company which assemble on the upper deck and talk, and walk, and smoke, and read, and meditate; while in the midst of the fluttering throng stands the square, sturdy figure of the man-at-the-wheel; his grave eye looking far ahead, and his weather-beaten face expressive of earnest attention to one paramount object—a striking contrast to those around, whose chief aim is to kill time.

The Bay of Biscay is now before us, but its crest-white dreaded waves have lost much of their terrors since steam has superseded wind. The calm that now broods upon the deep cannot delay us, as of yore, until a storm burst upon "our poor devoted bark," and hurl her, crushed and crippled, into port, or sink her in the brine. No! the ceaseless clank of our throbbing "heart" goes on, the clear waters are cleft, and a long line of foam marks our swift transit across the Bay of Biscay, as we pass Cape Finisterre and sweep down the coast of Portugal.

On our fifth day out we are on the *qui vive*, for we approach the first halting point on our long voyage. Cape St. Vincent is passed and the Spanish main comes into view. Here every bosom heaves with new and conflicting emotions, for Cape Trafalgar is before us, and thrilling recollections of England's greatest naval hero crowd the mind as we gaze upon the scene of England's irreparable loss and her greatest victory.

Beyond, on the horizon, rise the mountains of Africa, with Tangiers on the coast, and the next headland we pass reveals to us the flag of England as it waves its proud folds over the

ROCK OF GIBRALTAR.

It is a noble object in the midst of scenery of surpassing loveliness. The finely undulating and richly clothed hills of Spain, with Algesiras on the opposite side of the bay; the village of San Roque, on an eminence to the northward, overhung by a cork wood; the mountains of Granada in the distance; and the calm sea washing the low sandy tract called the neutral ground, at the extremity of which the bold Rock springs abruptly from the deep to a height of nearly 1500 feet, armed *cap-a-pie*, zig-zagged with pathways along its steep face, perforated with innumerable caverns, and bristling with upwards of a thousand cannon.

The Straits of Gibraltar, on which the fortress stands, extend upwards of thirty-six miles in length, and vary from twelve to twenty miles in width. This Strait is by no means commanded, as many suppose, by the Rock. The guns are nearly all turned westward, towards the Bay of Gibraltar, or northward, towards Spain. On the opposite shore frowns Mount Abyla, which, with the Rock of Gibraltar, acquired from the ancients the appellation of the Pillars of Hercules. Between these the tide of the Atlantic pours into the Mediterranean at the rate of five miles an hour.

The Rock is composed of limestone, and is perforated with innumerable caverns by nature as well as by man. Some of the latter are most wonderful, particularly those called the Galleries on the north front. Gibraltar is nearly three miles in length, and its breadth is not quite one mile. The ridge of rock is almost perpendicular on the eastern side—grand and gloomy—and across the neutral ground it rises like a solid wall, while towards the west it slopes more gradually. Here ranges of batteries rise from the sea along the entire front, tier above tier, while every crag and crevice, hollow and projection, bristles with artillery in a most imposing manner. All round the base, wherever there is an available spot, are perched white, sea-gull-looking houses, embosomed in many places in groves and gardens.

Half way up the western front are the white barracks and dwellings of the soldiers and many elegant villas, and towards the northern extremity lies the town.

In the magnificent Bay we drop anchor. As our stay is limited to twelve hours, and the objects of peculiar interest to be seen are, the Market, the Town, the Moorish Castle, the Galleries, the Alameda, and the view from the summit of the Rock—all of which require time—we must hasten on shore and be diligent, while we enjoy the balmy atmosphere of this delicious clime. Already it has told upon our fellow-passengers, who have doffed the thick habiliments of England and donned those of lighter material, more suited to the perfumed zephyrs of Spain. All are bent on enjoying to the full the brief space allowed them, so let us, reader, profit by their example, and do likewise.

The instant we set foot upon the quay, we are in the midst of a most motley group of earth's inhabitants ;—Jews, with their dark, grave, bearded faces; contrabandists, with their graceful broidered jackets; merchants, calculating prospective gains under the shadow of their sombreros; Turks and British soldiers, boatmen, jack-tars, porters, smugglers, and splendid-looking Moors from the coast of Barbary; all jostling each other, and the crowd of passengers who have just landed, and are gazing along with us at the gay and novel scene.

The Market, through which we have to pass on our way to the town, is situated between the first and second line of defences, and is usually crowded with a miscellaneous concourse, owing to its being traversed by the only road leading from the town to the Spanish lines. Here, during the morning hours, are to be seen the most splendid men and costumes in the world;—the dark Spaniard, with his tight jacket, crimson sash, broidered leggings, and conical hat—a costume admirably adapted to set off to advantage his robust, agile figure; the Moor—dignified, flowing, and magnificent, superior in deportment to his hereditary enemy and to all around him; the famous Spanish mantilla and fan, too, are seen here mingling their romantic influences with the eggs, poultry, and beef of Barbary. From the African coast Gibraltar is supplied with provisions, and the surrounding waters afford an abundant supply of excellent fish.

The Town itself is small and crowded, consisting of a few long, narrow streets, intersected by small lanes, which are so steep as to necessitate steps in order to ascend them. Of the old Moorish features of the Rock little remains, except the ruined Moorish Castle, which is an interesting and prominent object in the town. The houses, generally, are huddled together for want of room, and their rent is very high, and almost all the good ones are appropriated as "officers quarters."

Pressing onward we pass through the southern gateway of the town and emerge upon the Alameda—a most superb and singular promenade. It extends from the sea-wall to the foot of the steep Rock. Round three sides of it runs a pleasant walk shaded with trees, and at the southern extremity there is a garden with winding walks, bowers, and seats scattered throughout a mass of the richest verdure.

Here we may sit in the midst of clustering geraniums, blossoming and fruit-bearing orange trees, and aloes, and a multitude of creeping plants and sweet-scented flowers, absolutely bathed in perfume; whilst our eye embraces the blue Bay of Gibraltar, the mountains of Spain, the Straits dotted with white sails, the faint hills of Africa, and the distant Atlantic Ocean. Words cannot do justice to this noble prospect. But we must unwillingly tear ourselves away and ascend to the summit of the Rock.

The way up is zig-zag, as a matter of course, and trying to the limbs and lungs, but the view from the top well repays us for our trouble. Downwards we behold, with shrinking glance, a sheer descent of 1300 feet into the sea below. On the east the Rock presents a range of inaccessible precipices; on the west a gradual slope towards the crowded town, the suburbs with their villas and barracks, batteries, bastions, bay, and shipping. All around the uninterrupted eye sweeps in at a glance;—the Atlantic; the shores of Africa, with the walls of Tangiers on the Morocco coast; the spurs of Mount Atlas and Mount Abyla or Apeshill; the blue Mediterranean speckled with craft; and the mountains of Spain and Portugal; while the strains of military music from the band on the Alameda roll up the mountain side and mingle with the murmur of the town and shipping far below.

The early accounts of the Rock are somewhat confused. The Phœnicians, who regarded Gibraltar and its opposite partner the portals of the world, named it "Alube." The ancient Greeks called it "Calpe," and it was not until the invasion of Spain by the Moors that it received the name which has been corrupted into that borne by it at the present day. Tarik, with a force of 12,000 men, crossed the Straits and took the Rock after encountering slight opposition. Here he left a garrison, advanced into the interior, and gave the death blow to the Gothic empire in Spain. After this the Rock was known as *Gibel Tarik*, or the Mountain of Tarik, and time has modified this into Gibraltar!

That it is a place of great importance is evinced by the fact that it has stood thirteen sieges; and of these, four have occurred since it fell into the hands of the British in 1704. In that year it was taken by the English fleet, assisted by a body of 1800 men under the command of the Prince of Hesse D'Armstadt, and ever since it has remained under the

British crown, although many energetic attempts have been made by the Spaniards to regain the coveted stronghold. The last and most memorable siege commenced in June 1779, and lasted for three years and nine months, during which period the Rock was bombarded, almost without cessation, by the combined forces of France and Spain, both by land and by sea. The cannonading was at times terrific and the town was reduced to a heap of ruins; but no impression whatever could be made on the impregnable fortress, which, under General Elliot, the governor, with about 5380 men, offered a heroic and successful resistance.

There are two excellent libraries in the town, and several churches—Episcopal, Presbyterian, and Roman Catholic. The population, including the garrison, amounts to about 20,000 souls,—British, Spanish, Genoese, Jews, and Moors.

Thus much we have time to see and learn during our brief stay; but the signal is given, we hasten to the steamer, our iron heart throbs again, and away we go, sweeping out of the Bay, round Europa Point and into the beautiful Mediterranean. A long parting gaze we bestow upon Gibraltar as it drops a-stern, and then turn to the coast of Barbary.

And now, for a few days, we shall plough the blue waves of the Mediterranean. The sun is like a ball of fire in a shield of deepest blue, and our awning is found to be a most needful protection. Ceuta is passed on the right; on the left is seen the coast of Granada, which terminates in the white cliffs of Cape de Gatta. As we cleave our onward way, the coast of Algiers is seen faintly on our right, then Sicily rises to view; Cape Bon, on the African coast, glides past, and we approach the island of—

MALTA.

Our first thoughts are naturally of St. Paul—his perils on the deep and his landing on "Melita;" the reception he met with from the barbarians, and the miraculous cures which attested the divinity of the apostle's mission to preach "Christ crucified." But as we advance these thoughts are irresistibly swept away by the frowning, towering, bristling batteries of Valetta. It was a rude rock in possession of the Romans when Paul landed there; and as far as nature is concerned, it is not much more than a barren rock still, but on its rugged surface wealth and power have strewn many a luxury, and have built, perhaps, the strongest fortress in the world.

The group of islands which belong to the English consist of Malta, Gozo, and Comino—the last a small islet in the midst of the channel, of about five miles wide, that separates the two. Malta is about sixty miles in circumference, and contains upwards of 130,000 inhabitants. So barren is the limestone of which it consists, that the scanty supply of soil that exists has been imported thither from Sicily, and is banked up in terraces and husbanded with the greatest care. By dint of great exertion this soil is made to produce small quantities of sugar, oranges, indigo, and cotton; also corn sufficient for six months' consumption; all other supplies are imported.

There are many deep bays and excellent harbours on the shores of Malta, but none equal to the magnificent harbours of Valetta. The Great Harbour, towards which we hasten, is capable of containing upwards of a thousand vessels of the largest size, and is defended by tier upon tier of batteries that would bid defiance to the congregated fleets of the world. Valetta may be described as a bay full of fortified harbours, with a cape or tongue in the midst, on the point of which tongue is the city, and on its tip Fort Elmo; on the left is Fort Ricasoli; on the right Fort Tigné—all three guarding the entrance; while within the bay, point after point and battery after battery meet the eye in every direction.

The white lines of the fortifications cut sharply against the deep blue water and the sky, giving a terribly warlike aspect to the scene; which is further heightened by the numerous ships of war that we pass, and the red coats and the arms that gleam in the dazzling sunshine, and the constant clang of trumpet and roll of drum that fill our ears. The brilliancy and novelty of the scene are charming. Intermingled with the ponderous men-of-war are gaily painted, picturesque little boats, with white awnings, that dart hither and thither like beams of light. On shore are flat-roofed houses, so white that they appear to be cut out of the white rocks on which they stand. These are somewhat relieved by green balconies.

Landed on the stairs, we are instantly assailed by a rabble of pertinacious beggars, through whom we force our way up the steep ascent. In crossing the drawbridge our eye is arrested by the deep fosse, which is filled with orange-trees and bananas. Pressing on, we cross the well-filled and noisy market-place, and commence the toilsome ascent of one of the curious streets of stairs, for which Valetta is famous. But we must not take it too leisurely, for our stay here is to be only twenty-four hours.

Eliot Warburton says, in his own light and graphic way, "La Valetta is a sort of hybrid between a Spanish and an Eastern town; most of its streets are flights of steps, to which the verandahs are like gigantic banisters. Its terraced roofs restore to the cooped-up citizens all the ground lost by building upon, and there are probably not less than five hundred acres of promenadable roof in, or rather on, the city. The Church of San Giovanni is very gorgeous, with its vaulted roof of gilded arabesque, its crimson tapestries, finely carved pulpits, and its floor, which seems one vast escutcheon. It is a mosaic of knightly tombs, on which their coats of arms are finely copied in coloured marble and precious stones. The Chapel of the Madonna in the eastern aisle is guarded by massive silver rails, which were saved from French spoliation by being painted wood-colour. Amidst all this wealth and splendour, the proudest and most chivalric ornament of the church is a bunch of rusty old iron, suspended on the crimson tapestry. They are the keys of Rhodes, which the Order, overcome, but unconquered, carried away with them from their ancient seat, the bulwark of Christendom."

As we advance into the town, we are struck with the great variety and picturesqueness of the costumes that swarm around us;—the Maltese in his loose trousers, broad crimson sash, and shirt open at the collar, exposing his sunburnt neck and chest; the pale and unprepossessing priest; the grave Arab merchant from Tripoli; the hearty English sailor; the green-coated rifleman; the red-coated soldier; and the plumed Highlander, with his fluttering tartans; and last, though by no means least, the Maltese ladies, with their dark sparkling eyes, and their elegant black silk mantillas, which have the effect of rendering the plain pretty and the good-looking irresistible. Donkeys laden with merchandise ascend and descend these steep streets, which are lined with the stalls and workshops of the industrious population.

The chief points of interest to be visited in Valetta are, the far-famed Church of St. John, the Governor's Palace, the Armory, the Library, and the Museum; also the splendid view of the harbours and shipping from the Upper Baracca. After a glance at the main points of the city, and a saunter along the magnificent Strada Reale, we mount our ponies, and gallop away to take a view of Citta Vecchia, the ancient seat of the Knights Hospitallers. The road to it is barren and rocky, and the city itself a city of the dead. It is utterly deserted now. Not a sound is heard in the streets, in which the rank grass grows. The magnificent palaces and elegant houses are in good repair, but tenantless, and inexpressibly melancholy from the oppressive silence that reigns around. This was the ancient capital of the island, and the fortifications are of immense strength.

St. Paul's Bay is a little beyond Citta Vecchia. The Catacombs must be also visited; here, it is said, the early Christians were wont to worship. If time permits, we should take a walk over the fortifications. The strength of these strikes one more forcibly on a nearer inspection. Fort St. Elmo, in particular, is considered impregnable, and contains a treble row of bomb-proof magazines, capable of lodging two regiments of the line. One of the bastions on the extreme rocky point of Mount Sceberras contains the ashes of Sir Ralph Abercromby. The shortness of our stay forbids our lingering longer among these truly splendid fortifications, which are, at almost every point, memorable for the deeds of valour and endurance so often displayed by the warriors of modern times as well as by the chivalrous knights of old.

Malta was originally in possession of the Phœnicians, and afterwards fell successively into the hands of many different masters,—the Greeks, the Romans, the Goths, the Vandals, the Arabs, the Normans, the French, and the Spaniards. It was made over, by the Emperor Charles V., to the Knights Hospitallers of St. John, after they were driven from Rhodes.

In the fortress of Malta these knights were frequently besieged, and their valour and endurance on these occasions form the theme of some of the most spirit-stirring pages of history. Chief among their numerous Grand Masters rise the names of L'Isle, Adam, and La Valette. Internal dissensions sprang up amongst the knights in 1798, and they shamefully surrendered their stronghold to Napoleon Buonaparte without striking a blow. Thus ingloriously terminated an Order that had existed more than 700 years. The French, however, did not retain their conquest long. Shortly after Nelson's victory at Aboukir, the English fleet landed an army on the island, and established a blockade which lasted for two years. At length the French, after holding out to the last extremity, surrendered, and, in 1802, the British became the masters of Malta.

The island is the great quarantine station in the Mediterranean, and its fine climate has rendered it a favourite resort of invalids.

ALEXANDRIA.

There is little of interest to notice during our voyage from Malta to Alexandria. The sun shines brightly in the blue sky, and converts the ocean into a mass of heaving brilliants. Still the iron heart pants on, and the sharp prow of our fine vessel cleaves its eastward way; and the passengers, somewhat tired of sight-seeing and the bustle of Malta, recline lazily or saunter dreamily about under the awning which protects us from the fierce glare of the sun. On the morning of our fifteenth day from Southampton, we arrive at the ancient capital of Lower Egypt.

Alexandria is situated between the Lake Mareotis and the Isle of Pharos, and is enclosed within walls that are supposed to have been built by one of the successors of Saladin in the thirteenth century. The modern city is little better than a collection of half-ruined houses and rubbish, in the midst of which are to be seen the remains of a few of its ancient palaces. For a graphic description of this famous city let us again quote from the pages of Warburton :—

"All that is now visible within the shrunken and mouldering walls is a piebald town; one-half European, with its regular houses, tall, and white, and stiff; the other half Oriental, with its mud-coloured buildings and terraced roofs, varied with fat mosques and lean minarets. The suburbs are encrusted with the wretched hovels of the Arab poor; and immense mounds and tracts of rubbish occupy the wide space between the city and its walls; all beyond is dreary waste. Yet this is the site Alexander selected from his wide dominions, and which Napoleon pronounced to be unrivalled in importance. Here luxury and literature, the Epicurean and the Christian, philosophy and commerce, once dwelt together; here stood the great library of antiquity, 'the assembled souls of all that men held wise;' here the Hebrew Scriptures expanded into Greek under the hands of the Septuagint;

here Cleopatra revelled with her Roman conquerors; here St. Mark preached the truth upon which Origen attempted to refine, and here Athanasius held warlike controversy; here Amru conquered, and here Abercromby fell. Looking now along the shore, beneath me lies the harbour in the form of a crescent, the right horn occupied by the palace of the Pasha, his harem, and a battery; the left, a long low sweep of land, alive with windmills; the city in the centre: to the westward, the flat sandy shore stretches monotonously away to the horizon; to the eastward, the coast merges into Aboukir Bay."

The famous library above referred to was collected together in a somewhat singular manner. All the books brought into Egypt by foreigners were seized, and, without permission asked or obtained, were copied out by transcribers appointed for the purpose. The *originals* were then laid up in the library, and the *copies* were handed over to the proprietors! Little wonder that the library flourished and increased under such a system. It lay within the precincts of the Temple of Serapeum, and was composed of 700,000 volumes.

But to return to the modern city. The bay through which we pass is crowded with ships and boats, too curious and numerous to be described in brief, and, therefore, better left to the imagination, with this single remark, that all is impressively *Eastern*,—painted, gaudy, flowing, stately, turbaned, bearded, swarthy, and bathed in sweltering sunlight.

On landing, we find ourselves in the midst of crowds of sedate merchants, bales, ragged boys, camels, and donkeys, who create an effect upon our eyes and ears that is powerful, but by no means disagreeable, after our sea-voyage. We could, however, gladly dispense with the atrocious effluvia that greet our olfactory nerves, and make us wish for a blast of the fresh Mediterranean breeze.

However, mounted on our donkeys, we soon gallop through the filthy lanes of the Arab city, towards the *Grand Square* of the Frank quarter,—*vide*, our Engraving. Here dwell the consuls of the various European nations. The houses in the square are substantial, English-like, and elegant. Above their roofs towers an out-look, with an exposed spiral staircase. The motley crowd through which we pass is composed of Turks in their loose drapery, soldiers in white uniform, black slaves with picturesque crimson caps, and women, like ghosts, in garbs that conceal all save their eyes. Among these are heavily-laden camels, asses, and horses, some of the latter having richly embroidered saddles of crimson velvet.

As we have to spend a night in Alexandria, our first care, after securing beds, is to hire a donkey, and gallop to the principal sights. These are, the obelisk called Cleopatra's Needle, and Pompey's Pillar; the latter wonderful on account of its massive proportions. It was ascended by a party of British sailors, who attached a rope to the top of it by means of a kite. The Arsenal, the Pasha's Palace and Baths, are worthy of a visit. From Fort Cretin may be had an excellent view of the whole city.

Turning landward, we behold, with feelings almost approaching to solemnity, the ancient Nile, the mysterious river; the *cause* of the land of Egypt, and the ancient god of the Egyptians. Its waters, flowing from unknown regions in the far interior of Africa, have carried down the rich soil of Ethiopia, and deposited it, during the periods of annual inundation, on the barren desert, until that desert has bloomed like the gardens of paradise. Once a-year the river, owing to some cause known only to Him who created it, overflows its banks, spreading fertility over the fields, and carrying joy to the hearts of the people. In May it begins to rise; in August it is at its height, and Egypt is an archipelago. Then the waters gradually retire, and leave a deposit of mud on which the husbandmen plant and sow; the tropical sun vivifies all, and soon the land is clothed in green and gold.

Sweeping our glance over the city and the plain, we turn sea-ward, and here other and far different scenes are called to mind as we gaze at Aboukir Bay. On yonder line of deep blue water, amid the shoals, lay the splendid fleet of France at anchor. Into the offing the English fleet, with Nelson

Pompey's Pillar.

for its heart, sailed slowly, while at the mast head of the Admiral's ship flew the signal "close battle," and a British cheer rang over the wave as ship after ship ranged side by side with a Frenchman. The sun went down, but the lights of war sprang up, and the roar of quick artillery and the bursting crash of battle resounded all that night along the shores of Egypt.—But who knows not the story of the battle of the Nile? The morning came, and the rising sun revealed the fleet of France a group of blackened and dismasted hulls, with the flags of England waving over all.

Little more than two years later, and France once more contended here with England for the sovereignty of the East, but this time on the land. The shores of Aboukir Bay were girded with a wall of fire and bayonets, but British seamen pulled the oars, and British soldiers sprang upon the beach, and drove back the troops of France. A few days later, and the decisive battle was fought. On these plains the brave Abercromby led the English on to victory, and there the hero fell.

It was at this time that the dykes of the Lake Mareotis, then a fertile plain covered with habitations, were broken down; the sea burst in, and swept the whole away.

The population of Alexandria is about 20,000,—Arabs, Greeks, Europeans, Jews, Copts, &c. Its commerce is considerable, as all the imports to and exports from Egypt pass through it; and it has been of late much increased by extensive importations of cotton from that country. Not far from Pompey's Pillar is the canal by which water was brought from the Nile into the enormous cisterns beneath the city. These cisterns could only be filled at the periodical inundations of the Nile; and as there was no other supply of water for the city, they had to be constructed on an extensive scale. Although about 2000 years old, they are still perfect. A mile on the south side there are catacombs cut out of the rock,—a city of the dead, which some people may find pleasure in visiting.

The Palace of Cleopatra was built upon the walls facing the port. Of Cæsar's Palace only a few pillars and the front portico remain.

Alexandria was built by Alexander the Great, about 333

years B.C., soon after the fall of Tyre. He believed that the site was eminently appropriate as an emporium of the merchandise of the East and West. In this he was correct. It speedily grew and increased in wealth and splendour, until it became one of the most magnificent cities in the world. Pliny tells us that it was fifteen miles in circumference. It was intersected by straight parallel streets, and contained numerous temples and palaces of the most gorgeous description. The two principal streets formed a cross, and divided the city into four parts, forming a splendid square in the centre. The Palace, whose magnificence was increased by each successive Ptolemy, occupied a quarter of the city; and within its walls the body of Alexander the Great was deposited, in a golden coffin.

When in its zenith, Alexandria was only inferior to Rome itself in magnificence. It became the chief depôt of commerce between the East and West under the Ptolemys, and became a centre of Grecian art and science. Ptolemy Philadelphus added much to its grandeur, and built the famous watch-tower of Pharos, which was regarded as one of the wonders of the world. It was composed of white marble, and served as a beacon to guide sailors into port. In the year 141 B.C., Alexandria was almost destroyed by Ptolemy Physcon; at which time all the learned men fled to Greece, Asia Minor, and the islands of the Archipelago. The trade of the city began to decline after it fell into the hands of the Arabs, who burnt the celebrated library; and its fortunes were effectually blasted by the discovery of a route to India by the Cape of Good Hope, in 1499. Since that period its commerce has somewhat revived. Mehmet Ali, the late pasha, re-opened the canal, which had been choked up, and otherwise greatly improved the city.

Weeks might be spent here with pleasure and profit, for few cities present so many interesting features to our eye and memory. Its antiquities, its ruins, its former greatness, its desolation, all crowd upon our attention; but our time is short, the train is already panting,—that inexorable iron monster, which runs riot in the desert as rudely as in the peopled land, putting to flight, with its roar, the memories of the past, is waiting to whirl us off to Cairo. We leap in, and in a few moments leave Alexandria far behind us.

Until within a very recent period, the journey between Alexandria and Cairo used to be accomplished by canal to Atfech, where passengers embarked in a steamboat on the Nile, and were conveyed to Boulac; and thence, by omnibusses and asses, to the capital. Since the 1st of January 1856, however, travellers have been conveyed direct by railway.

The station of Kafr'el-Eis, which we pass, gives a fair idea of all the others on the same line. It is extremely simple in architectural appearance; has more the aspect of a workhouse than a station, and does not bear the least resemblance to those on European lines. The termini at each end are handsome and substantial. The porters on the line are astonishingly active fellows, and carry enormous burdens with the greatest apparent ease. An unsuccessful attempt has been made to get up a company to construct a ship-canal to connect the Mediterranean with the Red Sea, and thus enable vessels to pass from Western to Eastern waters without "breaking bulk." This would not interfere with the railway between Cairo and Suez, now approaching completion, as the latter is intended chiefly for passengers. The width of the desert isthmus between Cairo and Suez is about eighty miles, and it is at present traversed in rudely-constructed omnibusses.

At last we draw near to—

GRAND CAIRO,

Inseparably connected with Haroun Al Raschid of *Arabian Nights* celebrity; and, truly, this "El Kahira," this "city of victory," as it is styled by the Arabs, at the first glance almost realizes our youthful dreams. It was, however, the ancient city, about two miles from modern Cairo, which was, we presume, the scene of Haroun's adventures. It is now nearly uninhabited. The approach to the city from Boulac, the port, is superb. On the spur of the Mokattam mountain range rises the Citadel, with the purple hills in the background clearly defined against the glowing sky. Beneath, from out a sea of olives and acacia groves, springs the city, above the houses of which rise innumerable domes and minarets, the whole being enclosed by ramparts and towers partially hid from our view by the sycamore and fig trees that surround it. Mingling with the motley crowd, we push along, and gaze in wonder at the remarkable specimens of humanity around us. Here, we see camels marching along with stately step, and with slaves, black as coal, on their humps; ladies, like ghosts, in white; Turks and water-carriers; Europeans on asses and on foot; Arabs on mettlesome steeds, and stout merchants with pipes, turbans, and beards,—in short, the strangest mingling of Eastern and European costumes, faces, manners, and customs, that one could desire to behold.

But much of the illusory splendour of the city vanishes as we pass the gates, and traverse the labyrinth of narrow filthy lanes, into which only a subdued portion of light penetrates. We are instantly lost, and, but for our guide, would infallibly continue to wander in helpless despair. As we advance, crowds of villanous-looking dogs rush past, and threaten to trip us up, or rows of camels crush us against the houses, for the streets are nowhere more than twelve feet wide. Then comes a bridal procession; and after that a mountebank is seen delighting a crowd of children and beggars. Then a naked durweesh *demands* charity; and a water-carrier, with tinkling saucers, tempts you to drink.

All the streets of Cairo, however, are not narrow. There are one or two spacious squares, particularly Esbekeyeh, occupied by a large plantation and surrounded by a canal, round which runs a road shaded by palm and sycamore trees.

Here are the palaces of the pasha. Roumeleyeh is also a wide space, where fairs and markets are held. The bazaars are very interesting and varied. Each is devoted to a peculiar class of commodities; there are the jewellers' and armorers' quarters, and the Turkish, Persian, and Frank bazaars, where the stately shopmen sit in solemn silence, cross-legged on their counters, and smoking their pipes in apparently sublime indifference to trade.

A canal, named Khalis, traverses the city, and in its progress forms many small lakes or *berks*. The finest houses are on each side of this canal. It is dry during some months of the year, and covered with verdure; but when the Nile overflows, it is filled with water, and, Venice-like, the highway is crowded with barges and boats, while, at night, fireworks, music, and dancing, enliven the scene.

The houses of Cairo are for the most part lofty, built of mud and inferior brick, gloomy, windowless, and forbidding in appearance. The remarkable edifices all date from the reign of the Arabs and the ancient sultans of Egypt.

The most interesting building in the city is the *Citadel*, which was built by Saladin in the twelfth century. Let us hasten to it, for its battlements command a prospect of the utmost magnificence. On our way thither, we pass the *Mosque of Sultan Hassan*, an extremely light and elegant building, of great extent, and having a rich deep frieze round the top of the wall.

The scene that greets us as we mount the ancient walls of the Citadel is beyond description gorgeous. On one side, the rich plains of the land of Goshen stretching away to the horizon; on the other, the great desert, and the ancient, indestructible pyramids. Before are the ruins of Old Cairo, and the site of ancient Memphis; Djiah, the Obelisk of Heliopolis (the City of the Sun)—perhaps the oldest city in the land, and the school in which, it is said, Plato studied. All around are cities, and gardens, and olive groves, palm-forests, palaces, tombs, ruins, and luxuriant green fields, with the mysterious Nile flowing in the midst of this land ot its own creating. But let us turn from the view for a mo-

Mosque of Sultan Hassan.

ment, and regard the spot where the last of the heroic Mamelukes escaped from the treachery of Mehmet Ali.

To this Citadel the pasha summoned the Mameluke beys to a consultation in reference to the approaching war with the Wahabees in Arabia, and, at the same time, invited them to a feast. The Mamelukes came mounted on their finest horses, and clad in their magnificent uniform, and a more splendid body of cavalry the world never saw. After the feast, the pasha requested them to parade in the court of the Citadel. They did so, unsuspectingly; but no sooner had the last horseman passed, than the portcullis fell. Instantly they became aware that their doom was sealed; a single glance showed that they were hopelessly enclosed within blank insurmountable walls, and soon after a blaze of musketry from the ramparts above began the work of death. The brave Mamelukes met their fate like heroes. Many of them crossed their arms upon their bosoms, and bent their heads in prayer, while volley after volley poured down on their devoted heads, and strewed the court-yard with the dead. All fell save one,—Emin Bey—who was, we may almost say, miraculously preserved in the midst of a tempest of bullets. Spurring his charger over a heap of his slaughtered comrades, he leaped upon the ramparts. One frantic bound from the dizzy height, and the noble steed fell with a crash to the earth,—another moment, and the daring Mameluke sprang from his dying horse, and fled amid a shower of bullets. He escaped into the deserts of the Thebaid.

The Necropolis of Cairo is well worthy of a visit. The desert towards the east is studded with mausoleums and sepulchres, on which large sums have been lavished. These present a very striking and singular effect to a European eye, especially the cemetery of the pasha.

The *Tombs of the Mamelukes*, a short distance from the city, were in former days, fine specimens of Egyptian architecture. Our Engraving represents their appearance before the hand of time had reduced them to the few remains that now exist.

About a mile in another direction are the *Tombs of the Caliphs.* They are light, elegant structures, in the Saracenic style of architecture; and there is some exquisite work on the domes and minarets. We must not omit a visit to the

Tombs of the Mamelukes.

Slave Market. It is not easy to obtain admission to that part of the market where the white slaves of Georgia and Circassia are sold, in consequence of the insults that have frequently been heaped on the slave-dealers by indignant Europeans; but there is no difficulty in gaining admission to the court of the African slaves, who are regarded as inferior cattle. Alas, for the wretched land where woman is bought and sold!

In *Old Cairo,* we are shown the *Granaries of Joseph,* and *Joseph's Well.* There is little else of interest here, except, indeed, the varieties of oddly costumed natives and travellers one meets with on the banks of the Nile. If time permits, we may extend our excursions to the following places: *Memphis,* of which little remains but the Mummy Pits and a few scattered ruins; the *Obelisk of Heliopolis,* supposed to have been erected by the Pharaoh of Joseph's time,—a three hours' ride; the *Gardens of Rhoda;* and the Palace of the Pasha at Shoubra.

The Pyramids of Ghizeh and the *Sphinx* we have not yet mentioned, as they merit special and separate notice. Furnished with Arab guides and donkeys, and whips of portentous dimensions, we canter forth. Some energetic travellers set out in the afternoon with a supply of provisions and candles, in order to spend the night there and sleep in a tomb, that they may have the satisfaction of seeing the sun rise from the summit of Cheops, as the Great Pyramid is called. We prefer a bed in our hotel, therefore we start in the morning.

As we near these mighty artificial mountains, we become gradually impressed with their enormous size. There are three—that of Cheops being the largest. It is about 500 feet in height, and covers a space of ground equal to eleven English acres. The stones of which it is built are of enormous size, and when we consider that such ponderous blocks were brought from the quarries of Toura, on the opposite side of the Nile, probably without the aid of any machinery, save that of the simplest kind, we may form some idea of the immense labour that must have been expended on their construction.

Pyramids of Ghizeh.

With the aid of two Arabs we scramble up the gigantic steps of Cheops. Truly it is no light work, and on reaching the half-way resting place our British blood—boiling already from exertion—is suddenly set on fire by the traitorous guides who coolly refuse to go a step farther with us unless we give them *backsheesh*. For a moment our fists involuntarily double, and the vision of two Arabs rolling head-over-heels down that terrific flight of stairs floats before us; then reason steps in, our hand wanders slowly to our breeches pocket, *backsheesh* is produced, and we continue our ascent. Breathless and panting we gain the summit—in attempting which feat not a few travellers have been killed—and from the little platform on that giddy height cast our eyes abroad upon the land of Egypt. The romance of life is being gradually banished from our world. Even here, by the deserts of Africa, in the ancient land of the Pharaohs, we are compelled to remember the common-place fact that the Pyramids are *farmed out*. Yes, they are actually rented from the pasha, like an English toll-bar! In the interior are several chambers and passages, all of which we visit in due course, and listen, if so disposed, to the explanatory discourse of our conductor.

The Sphinx is very much drifted up with sand, as indeed are also the Pyramids. It is of enormous size, and many years ago was cleared to its foundation by a Mr. Caviglia, who found its huge legs stretched out fifty feet in advance from the body, and the remains of a temple between its paws.

In returning to Cairo we visit the Isle of Rhoda.

Of the history of Cairo we have not space to say more than that it was founded in the tenth century, by Jawhar, a Moggrebin general, and soon became the capital of Egypt. The population is upwards of 300,000. There are several khans and caravansaries, which are always full of people and merchandise, Cairo being the great centre of the trade of the interior of Africa, and the seat of government.

Shepherd's hotel is the best in the city.

Having seen the wonders of Grand Cairo, we resume our journey, which now lies across—

THE DESERT OF SUEZ.

The distance is between 80 and 90 miles, and is performed in omnibusses and on camels. But this route is on the eve of a great change. Even while we write, the "iron horse" snorts in rapid flight across the sandy waste in its trial trips; the wires of the electric telegraph cut against the deep-blue sky, and the retreating posts, growing "small by degrees and beautifully less," disappear in long perspective on the golden horizon; a few brief weeks and the old system of buss' and camel shall have retired into the past;—but ere it goes, and while yet a few grains of sand remain in its hour-glass, let us describe it still as "the route across the desert."

There are six omnibusses of somewhat rude construction, mounted on two wheels, and capable of holding six inside. Two Nubians drive—one being a sort of guard, mender of broken traces, and restrainer of fiery steeds; and, truly, the steeds need restraining. There are four: the wheelers are mules; the leaders, little mettlesome Arabs, which can scarcely be held in,—and no wonder, for the imps of darkness who yell and hoot around us as we prepare to start, and the shouts of the miscellaneous and swarthy throng, are too much for these half-tamed steeds of the desert. The mules are sedate. They heed not noise and confusion; yet they can go—ay, as fleetly as the leaders, though they make less fuss about it.

Our Nubians,—bare-footed, bare-legged, and bare-armed, with loose blue blouses and white caps—are active as monkeys, wild as zebras. They leap on the box; the crowd scatters right and left; the crack of the whip is drowned in a torrent of yells; out we sweep through the gates of Cairo, and dash like one of its own whirlwinds across the sandy desert.

There are no suburbs to this part of Cairo. The city and the desert stand in defiant juxtaposition, so that, in ten minutes, we leap from the busy heart of the one, and find ourselves flying over the arid solitudes of the other. There is not much of a road, and our reckless drivers mind it but little, in consequence of which we sometimes stick in the sand,—affording an opportunity to the English to grumble, and exhibit their strength of muscle in extricating the vehicle, while the Nubians stamp and yell and lash the horses, until by dint of bursting efforts it is got out and we proceed.

Driving in the desert is no neat-handed, gentle operation. There is no tenderness exhibited towards the cattle. We start at full gallop, and a courier precedes us. If any unfortunate driver cannot keep up with the others he is certain to receive a visit and a sharp rebuke from that individual; so that the cattle arrive at each station panting and flecked with foam. There are seven stations, at each of which horses are changed. Ten minutes suffice to perform this operation, during which interval we get out, stretch our cramped legs and watch the busy scene. The air is terribly sultry; we almost fall into a doze while gazing abstractedly at a group of mild-faced camels, on whose backs our luggage is strapped, and we begin a dreary speculation as to the appropriateness of the costume of several black-faced, bright-eyed Bedouin Arabs beside them, when we are suddenly roused by a shout; we step into our buss, but forgetting the absurd formation of the vehicle, which necessitates our stepping *down* as if into a hole, we fall prostrate amongst the feet of our laughing companions, and ere we have regained our seat, the fresh steeds are bounding at full stretch over the sandy plain as if the ghowls of the desert were yelling in pursuit.

Dead camels, which have perished in crossing, are seen in all stages of decomposition on our track, with surfeited vultures in solemn torpidity beside them. Sometimes a band of wandering Bedouins, armed to the teeth, sweep past us—wild as they were in the days of old when Joseph sojourned in the land of Egypt, and only restrained from appropriating our possessions from a salutary dread of the pasha's soldiery. Here and there we pass a long string of camels, or the tomb of some rich Arab who has died on his pilgrimage to Mecca, or a few stunted shrubs, which, all insignificant though they be, if compared with other and more favoured plants, are nevertheless beautiful and refreshing *here.* Sundry telegraph towers, too, set up to notify the approach of caravans, enliven the desert, so that it is by no means so monotonous as we had anticipated.

At certain of the stations twenty or thirty minutes are allowed us for rest and refreshment. All the arrangements connected with these are most admirable; and appearing, as they do, suddenly in the midst of desolation, cause a powerful feeling of gratitude to the Pasha and the Transit Administration Company to arise in our hearts. The chief of these is—

THE CENTRAL STATION IN THE DESERT,

A square, clumsy, ungainly mass of building, into which we drive, hot and cramped and thirsty. Under such circumstances can you wonder that we doubt the evidence of our senses, and fancy that somehow we have got into an *Arabian Nights'* dream, when we behold champagne, pale ale, and bottled stout, in abundance? The viands are good, and supplied by the Transit Administration at the rate of three meals per diem; but drinkables are charged extra. However, they are very moderately valued and most acceptable.

This station is provided with every convenience—beds, couches, and large refreshment rooms. The station-rooms here are all alike—square, white-washed, stone-floored, with a divan running round the room and a table in the middle. Here we lave our parched hands and faces in cold water, put on our veils to protect our eyes from the sand, hoist our umbrella,—which, by the way, ought to be termed a *parasol* —and saunter out while refreshments are preparing. Camels are kneeling quiescently,—patient, mild animals they are, a perpetual rebuke to the men who grumble and shout and fume around them! There are goats also,—an ill-looking dog or two,—a few cocks and hens;—the now empty omnibusses, tilted up for want of horses to keep them straight on their single axle-trees. Besides this—nothing, save the hot desert and the blazing sun. It is generally thought advisable to drink as little water as possible on this journey. Brandy and pale ale, especially the latter, are the staple beverages. The former is useful to prevent cramp in the stomach, to which travellers are liable on account of the heat by day and the cold dews by night.

Rested, refreshed, and fortified within, we spring forward once more with renewed vigour, and, if possible, increased noise among the drivers, and thus onward we fly for fifteen hours, passing station after station until at last we draw near to Suez. Here a feeling of solemnity steals over us as we behold the range of *Mount Sinai* in the far distance, and call to remembrance the momentous events that were transacted there. But, alas! no such feelings influence our wild conductors. They dwell near to the scene where the Almighty wrought miracles of the most awful and convincing nature before the eyes of men, but they believe not, and the only feeling in their mind as they come in sight of Suez and descry the mail packet at anchor off the bay, is one of intense desire each to outstrip his comrades in the race. They dash off the beaten road in their eagernes, fly over sandy ridges and stony ground as if they desired to smash the vehicles, and at length terminate our anxieties and the journey by sweeping at full gallop into—

SUEZ.

Fifteen hours' almost incessant galloping and jolting over the parched desert is a good preparative for the beautiful and refreshing view of the *Red Sea*, at the head of which this miserable town is situated.

By railway the journey from Cairo to Suez will be shortened to less than three hours—whereby, no doubt, much valuable time will be saved and much discomfort avoided; nevertheless, a great deal of enjoyment will be lost when the old route and method are forsaken. The chief engineer on the line is M. A. Monchelet, and it is constructed at the expense of the Egyptian government.

There is nothing worthy of notice in Suez except Shepherd's hotel, from the verandah of which we enjoy a fine view of the Red Sea and a cigar, and watch the numerous boats that enliven the scene before us. But we may not sit in contemplation long, for the Transit Administration do not put themselves to much trouble with our luggage, beyond carrying it, and we may find that there is something to pay for overweight. This we must ascertain for ourselves at the Transit Office—in the hotel—as they won't tell us, and, if not paid for, the package will be detained.

The town is built on a low sandy tract of land, and the heat and glare of the sun are very oppressive. In fact the place is so wretched that we shall hasten away from it as fast as we can. The population is about 8,000. Caravans start from hence across the desert twice a-day.

Let no traveller omit to lay in a stock of oranges here. The voyage down the Red Sea is most trying to *every* constitution, owing to the unbearable heat. Pale ale and oranges are *life* in such a caldron, in which not a few Europeans perish both on the outward and homeward voyage. Some people recommend aperient draughts occasionally. We simply state the fact, having no opinion on that subject!

A small tug steamer conveys us to the mail packet; the anchor is weighed, and we are steaming swiftly down the

RED SEA.

But the Red Sea is not red,—it is not even blue; it is green,—bright green, owing to its shallowness; which cause compels us to steer carefully in the centre. It is calm and beautifully soft, and the sinking sun brings out the sharp ridges of the hills, and throws the ravines into deeper shade.

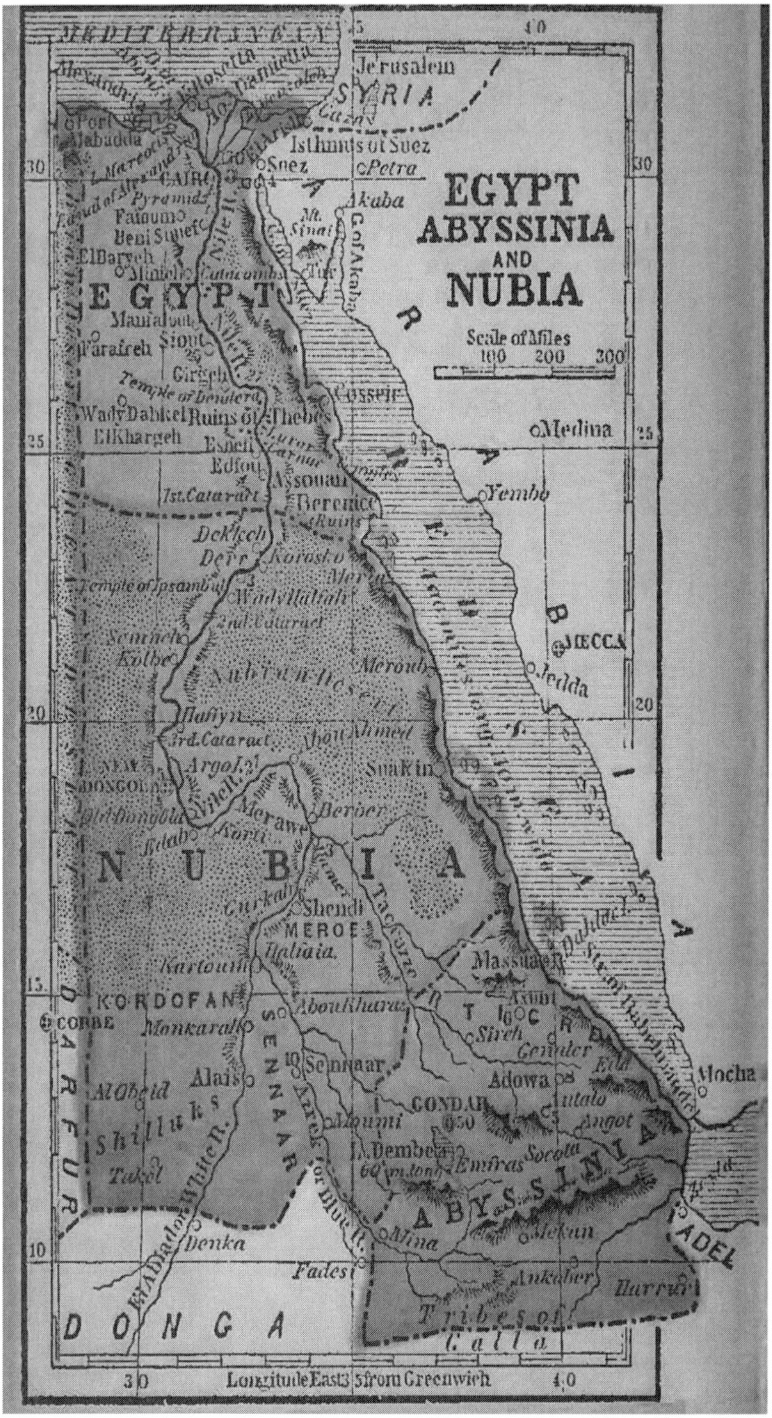
EGYPT
ABYSSINIA
AND
NUBIA
Scale of Miles
100 200 300
Jerusalem
SYRIA
Isthmus of Suez
Suez
Petra
Akaba
Mt. Sinai
CAIRO
Pyramids
Faioum
Beni Suief
El Daryeh
Minieh
Catacombs
EGYPT
Manfalout
Siout
Farafreh
Girgeh
Temple of Dendera
Wady Dakhel
Ruins of Thebes
El Khargeh
Esneh
Edfou
Assouan
Berenice
1st Cataract
Korosko
Temple of Ipsambul
Wady Halfah
2nd Cataract
Semneh
Kolbe
Medina
Yembo
MECCA
Jedda
Hafiyr
3rd Cataract
Abou Ahmed
Suakin
Berber
Merawe
NUBIA
Shendi
MEROE
Kartoum
Massuah
Axum
KORDOFAN
COBBE
Monkarah
Sennaar
Adowa
GONDAR
Alais
Al Obeid
Mocha
Angot
Socota
ABYSSINIA
Emfras
Denka
Fadasi
Ankober
Harrur
ADEL
Tribes of Galla
DONGA
DARFUR
Longitude East 35 from Greenwich
30
40
25
20
15
10

The Arabs call the Red Sea Bahr-Malak, or the Salt Sea,—a much more appropriate name than the other.

The shores of the Gulf of Suez are table-land, about 3000 feet high on either side, and the view of Suez on looking back is rather picturesque, Mount Sinai being the most interesting as well as most prominent object in the scene. The Red Sea is about 1300 miles long and 200 broad, and is full of coral reefs. About half way between Suez and Aden, we pass between two remarkable rocks named the *Two Brothers.* Few vessels are seen on the way,—a boat or two, perhaps, conveying pilgrims to Mecca. As we near the Straits of Babel Mandeb, Mocha,—of coffee celebrity—is visible on the left. The Island of Perim, which we pass, is an important possession of the East India Company, as it commands the entrance to the Red Sea. There is a temporary fortification on it, and supplies are carried thither from Aden—the island being barren. On our fifth day from Suez we descry the conical peaks of—

ADEN,*

And, soon after, we drop anchor in the harbour. This is a great coaling station, at which vessels from England land coals, and proceed to India nd Australia in search of freight. On casting anchor we immediately jump into a boat, and are rowed by four savage-looking red-haired Arabs (arrant knaves) to the hotel on the beach. It is the best building in the town, having a sheltering verandah round it, and all the comforts we can desire.

At this point in the journey travellers ought to make particular inquiries as to their future proceedings, because Aden is a centre from which different vessels diverge, to the Mauritius, the various ports in India, Ceylon, and China. Mak-

* Our views of Aden and Madras are copied, by the kind permission of the Directors of the Peninsular and Oriental Steam Navigation Company, from pictures in their possession.

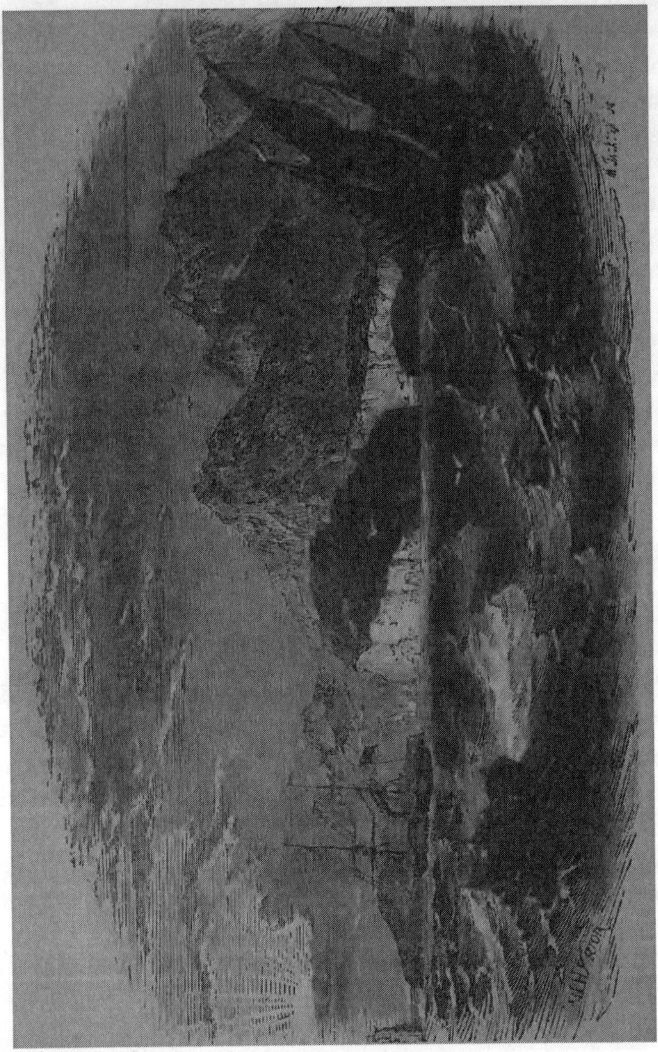

Aden from the Sea.

ing these inquiries, taking his passage, changing his vessel, and refreshing his over-heated frame, will occupy the traveller a large part of the few hours spent here in coaling, so that he will have little time for sight-seeing. Fortunately this is a matter of small moment, as there are no sights to see! Aden is not particularly interesting. It is chiefly remarkable for its barren, bluish-coloured hills, on the highest of which—Signal Hill—we observe a signal post. The houses are built of bamboo, and on a foundation of sand. Four miles in the interior is the Turkish Wall, where the British military force is situated. Should we find time to wander about we will be much amused with the sheep here, whose tails are so fat as sometimes to weigh above 9 lbs.; and should we treat ourselves to a chop, we shall find to our satisfaction that they make excellent mutton. Fruit, rice, coffee, mutton, &c., are brought hither by the Arabs. The population of the place is about 20,000, and the water they drink execrable; therefore, as you value your health, cling to oranges, pale ale, and soda water. In regard to Aden this is all; and all this we quit without a sigh, and embark for an eight days' voyage on the Arabian Sea. The best view, perhaps, of Aden and its fortifications is had from the steamer as we sail away,—like an unwelcome visitor, who appears most agreeable to our eyes when retreating.

And now, another dash over the briny deep. For little more than a week the sun of the torrid zone pours down on our vessel, and we arrive at—

BOMBAY.

The harbour here is capable of containing upwards of a thousand sail. The Island of Bombay, on which the city is built, is situated on the western coast of Hindostan. It is about eighteen miles in circumference, and formed part of the portion paid with the Infanta of Portugal to Charles II., by whom it was given to the East India Company. Since then it has become an important British station, and gives its name to one of the three presidencies into which Hindostan is divided.

The view, as we steam into the harbour, is very picturesque; and its beauty is doubtless enhanced in our eyes, in consequence of the length of time we have passed on the boundless ocean. On the right are beautiful green hills studded with cottages and villas,—bungalows, as they are called here,—around which grow in luxuriant profusion the shrubs and gorgeous flowers of this gorgeous land. On the left lies the fort, with its powerful batteries and numerous buildings, and in the distant background the mighty Ghauts rear their summits to the skies.

As soon as the anchor is let go we leap into a bunder boat, and alight at the foot of a flight of stone steps, named Apollo Bunder, by which we ascend to the city. At the top of these a formidable battery confronts us with a sardonic grin, and numerous palanquins await us. Throwing ourselves into one of these portable beds, we recline at full length, and are borne off by four black fellows to a hotel, from which we afterwards proceed to see the city. And a strange sight it is in many respects.

The dockyard, the fort, the bazaars, the Hindoo temples, and innumerable other buildings, claim our attention, but can scarce obtain it, owing to its being already fixed on the motley population. English, French, Americans, Portuguese, Parsees, Chinese, Arabs, Armenians, Abyssinians, Hindoos, Greeks, and soldiers, both British and native, infantry and cavalry, &c. &c.,—all in national costume,—jostle each other in the crowded streets in most picturesque confusion. The places of interest in Bombay are far too numerous to mention, but the visitor will have no difficulty in finding them out.

Bombay is the station of the Indian navy and the headquarters of the Bombay army. The latter is composed chiefly of native troops, officered by Europeans. The population is about 570,000. There is telegraph communication with all the chief places in India. The principal article of export is cotton. The island is low, and, therefore, rather unhealthy. Lowest range of the thermometer is 52°, highest 140°.

In order to touch at Bombay we have led our traveller slightly out of the direct route to China, which lies straight across the sea from Aden to—

POINT DE GALLE—CEYLON.

This is the next halting point in our voyage. From Ceylon steamers leave on the 1st of every month for Bombay, and on the 1st and 18th for England, by way of the Red Sea; for Madras, Calcutta, and China, on the 7th and 24th of every month; the royal mail steamers for Australia arrive here from Suez on the 14th, and arrive, homeward-bound, on the 8th of each month: so that this island is a bustling, business-like place, as well as a "terrestrial paradise," as the natives style it. Like most other terrestrial paradises, Ceylon has seen a good deal of terrestrial fighting in its day. After a long period of intermitting peace and war, among natives, Portuguese, Dutch, and English, the island was finally ceded to the latter in 1815, and has since continued under British rule. It is situated in the Indian Ocean, near Cape Comorin; is 270 miles long, 150 broad, has a population of about 1,130,000, and is exceedingly rich and beautiful,—as the view in our Engraving, taken from a point inland, will show. Our vessel stops twenty-four hours here to take in coal, so we have time to see a little of the island. The fort and various public buildings are worth visiting. There are several cities and towns in the interior, in one of which (Candy) is a public library, erected on pillars and built in a lake. The highest hill on the island, Adam's Peak, is 3200 feet in height. Hither pilgrims flock to see the supposed impression of Buddha's foot in the rock. Off the north-west of Ceylon is a great and valuable pearl fishery.

The natives are of Hindoo origin. The products are pepper, cinnamon, cotton, silk, ivory, ebony, musk, crystal, saltpetre, sulphur, lead, iron, copper, gold, silver, all kinds of precious stones except diamonds, fish and fowl, cocoa-nuts, cattle, fruits, vegetables, and wild animals, especially elephants, which are remarkably numerous. Under British rule Ceylon has advanced and prospered much, and it is at present proposed to connect it by submarine telegraph with Madras, Bombay, and Calcutta.

Once more on the deep. For four days we cleave the waves of the Indian Ocean; then the Coromandel coast is neared, and we reach—

MADRAS.

We will not weary the reader with minute details here. The following brief summary of facts, and the view given in our Engraving, will prepare the traveller to land and enjoy himself.

Madras is the capital of the presidency of that name, and is situated in the Carnatic, on the shore of the Bay of Bengal. The shore is so low that the approach is somewhat dangerous, and the landing can only be effected in native barges, called massoollah boats. These are well manned, however, and skilfully handled, so that we dash through the heavy swell and foaming surf in safety. When the surf is too much for these boats, another species of craft called catamaran is used. It is advisable to wear spectacles on landing, to protect the eyes from the intense glare of the sun on the yellow houses.

On the beach stands Fort St. George (the original name of the station), a fortress of great strength. The public edifices, —also on the beach,—including the custom-house and court-house, are very fine buildings. The city is divided into two, —the White Town and the Black Town; so called from the complexion of their respective inhabitants. The Europeans reside in scattered bungalows in the midst of gardens. The principal buildings, besides those alluded to above, are St. George's Church, Government House, Madras Club, the College, &c. The only object in the vicinity worth visiting is St. Thomas's Mount.

Buggies ply like cabs in England, so that we can be easily conveyed through the various parts of Madras in a few hours.

The population of Madras is above 400,000. Hotels are bad, but the club excellent. Railways are opened into the interior, and advancing rapidly. Electric telegraph to Bombay and Calcutta. Lowest range of thermometer is 75°, highest 140°. Thus much,—and a great deal more that must be seen to be fully appreciated,—we learn as we drive through the burning streets of Madras; and we are by no means sorry when, after due refreshment at the excellent club-house, we find ourselves once more on board our ocean house, and steaming away for—

CALCUTTA.

Less than three days brings us to the mouth of the river Hooghly, up which we steam for 100 miles ere we anchor off the Gauts of this city of palaces,—the seat of government of the Bengal presidency and the capital of British India.

Wonderful and striking is the change as we rush suddenly from the bosom of the briny ocean into the majestic river. On each side the banks, in some places very high, are covered with luxuriant tropical vegetation,—the golden and sweet-scented babool, the magnolia, the graceful bamboo, and a host of other beautiful plants and trees, springing out of dense shrubbery. Here we begin to feel more powerfully than we have yet done that we have reached the famous land of India; and every object that meets our wondering gaze tends to deepen and intensify this feeling, which is at length brought to a climax by the sudden appearance of the magnificent city.

Calcutta stands on the east bank of the Hooghly, a branch

of the Ganges. It is upwards of six miles in length, extending along the river's bank. The population is about 600,000, and, like the other principal cities under British rule, of a very mixed character, affording the stranger no small amount of amusement in the way of costume and physiognomy. Many of the houses are tall and stately, with verandahs and Grecian pillars. Behind the front lines of mansions is the native town, with dirty, narrow streets, dirty natives,—all more or less naked,—ghastly religious mendicants, showy marriage processions, and sounds of creaking wheels and discordant voices. From the quay, built by Lord Hastings, we may see all this, and also the vessels of every shape and size from all parts of the world; while near the banks are hundreds of Brahmins, saying their prayers and washing in the deified river.

This is a great commercial city. The river is deep and broad,—fully a mile at Calcutta,—and the tributaries of the Ganges afford facilities for trade with the rich interior; consequently the traffic is very great, and the population of the surrounding country is dense. Hotels are large and numerous. Railways and electric telegraphs connect the city with many important stations inland. The lowest range of the thermometer is 52°, highest 140°.

The buildings, &c., worth seeing are too numerous to particularize. Our Engraving gives the view from Garden Reach, and embraces the river Hooghly, with its crowd of shipping and boats. The splendid new *Government House,* in the centre, was built by the Marquis of Wellesley; and *Fort William,* to the right, was begun by Lord Clive. It is the strongest fortress in India, used to be garrisoned by two or three European regiments and native troops; but since the terrible mutinies of the present year (1857), it is probable that important changes will be made in regard to this. To the left of the Government House are seen the handsome buildings of the *Esplanade.* The gauts, or broad flights of steps on the banks of the river, are curious; and the pagodas, temples, &c., are absolutely innumerable and totally indescribable.

In order to visit Madras and Calcutta we have again diverged from the direct route to China. From Point de Galle the steamer proceeds straight east, until it cleaves the islet-studded waves of the Malacca Straits. After a voyage of five days from Point de Galle we touch at—

PENANG,

Or, the Prince of Wales Island. This is the seat of government of the British possessions in the Straits of Malacca; a very fine island, mountainous, comparatively cool and salubrious. It is 18 miles long by 8 broad, and was purchased by the East India Company in 1786. It lies on the west coast of Malay. Population is about 40,000. Our time here is short, and, after a few hours' halt, we proceed on our rapid course through the interesting Straits of Malacca towards—

SINGAPORE.

The voyage from Penang to Singapore occupies two days, and is varied and pleasant, as land is in sight all the way. The bold mountain ranges of the Malay peninsula appear on our left, and the picturesque islets of the straits, with the Island of Sumatra, on our right.

Singapore, alias Lion's Town, is at the southern extremity of the Malay peninsula, and the population is upwards of 60,000. It stands on a small island about 80 miles distant from the equator. A strait, quarter of a mile wide, divides it from the mainland. The town is built on a salt creek which can only be navigated by boats, and the ship anchorage is two miles from the town. A chain of small islands, seaward of Singapore, are inhabited by a race of semi, if not absolute, savages, of whom little is known. The settlement is a British possession, and was founded in 1819 by Sir Stamford Raffles.

Being a great entrepôt for merchandise passing between Europe and Asia, the harbour is constantly alive with vessels and craft of all kinds, taking their departure for, or arriving from all parts of the world. The climate is excellent,—so much so, as to have obtained the name of the "Paradise of India." Here day and night are equal, the sun rising at 6 A.M. and setting at 6 P.M. Rains fall moderately; there is little variation in the temperature, and extreme summer heat and winter cold are unknown. Paradise though it be, however, we must leave it, and continue our voyage for eight days through the China Sea towards—

HONG-KONG.

This part of the voyage is exceedingly interesting, and the wooded mountain ranges on shore most beautiful. At the mouth of the Tigris (Si-Kiang) especially, the scenery and fortified hills are extremely picturesque.

Here, then, we are at length in the land of "Tchou-Koue," the "centre of the earth," the land of exclusiveness, opium, pigtails, and tea. The island of Hong-Kong is a British settlement of recent growth. It was ceded to the English, along with £5,000,000, at the peace of 1842, as indemnification for the expenses of the war. The principal fort, Victoria, is about a mile in extent, and lies at the entrance of the Canton river. The approach to it is very picturesque, and everything that meets the eye has something brilliant or grotesque, or both, about it. The town is about a mile in extent, and among the objects of interest we may mention the government offices; the painters' workshops; the shawl manufactories; and the shops of the carvers of wood, ivory, and tortoise-shell.

But everything that we behold is a "sight," and we shall find endless amusement in rambling through the crowded streets where the Chinese, with shaved heads and pigtails, and clad in their loose and dirty garments, prosecute their various trades in the open air. Bustling animation, business, and confusion, seem to reign in the streets, and also on the water, where men-of-war and merchantmen mingle with junks, and barges, and boats, that almost defy description, and seem the very extreme of nautical absurdity! Some of these are of great size. Some have preposterously high sterns with windows and galleries; others have houses on deck, like toy Noah's-arks; gay streamers and flags fly from the disproportioned masts; enormous eyes are painted on the bows; and clumsy, curiously-formed sails are hoisted to the breeze. Flower boats, or floating nurseries, perfume the air; and paint of the most gaudy colour is distributed profusely over everything. In short, the whole scene has more the appearance of an overgrown toy-shop than a sober picture in real life.

Above the town, at West Point, we see the rocky hill called Possession Peak, rising almost perpendicularly; and the narrow belt of available building ground is covered with houses of white freestone. The place is in a very prosperous condition, despite its unhealthy character, and the population is about 25,000. The summer is oppressively hot and the winter very cold, July and August being the hottest months of the year.

Once more we advance, and about 280 miles farther on, touch at the island of—

AMOY.

The sights of this place are very similar to those in Hong-Kong. The port is a fine one, capable of containing 1000 sail. The population 30,000; circumference fifteen miles. Passing onward from this island, about which there is nothing particularly interesting, we continue our course 520 miles farther, and finally terminate our long voyage at—

SHANGHAI.

This is the most northerly Chinese port open to European trade, is a good harbour, and has a very extensive commerce. It stands on the banks of the Woosung river, about twenty-five miles from its mouth, and vessels of large burthen can approach the city. The population is 60,000. There are several good hotels, and a public tea garden in the vicinity, which is much frequented. The harbour is crowded with junks, and the spacious wharves and warehouses with merchandise, indicating the immense traffic of the port. The houses are low and the streets narrow, but some of the principal buildings and temples are magnificent. The fine yellow cotton used in the manufacture of Nankin cloth is grown in abundance here.

There are many remarkable objects in this city; among others we may mention the city wall and its fine gates, the tea factories, the English cemetery, and the extensive suburbs. Indeed, we may include among remarkable objects the entire population, and all their curious, and we its fain to add, absurd costumes and customs.

Shanghai is the *ultima Thule* of our voyage and of British intercourse with China. Beyond this the mails proceed in farther; therefore, courteous reader, we bid thee farewell, and wish you an agreeable sojourn in foreign lands and a pleasant voyage home.

GENERAL INFORMATION AND ADVICE.

Let the traveller, as an essential preliminary step, foreign himself with the *Hand-book of Information* published he the Peninsular and Oriental Steam Navigation Company, as 122 Leadenhall Street, London; and Oriental Place, South ampton: and if he would save himself much time, Steam and inconvenience, let him carefully attend to *all* him if contains.

Take with you as little luggage as possible, and be careful to comply with the Company's regulations as to size. On every package, however small, see that you get a printed "destination label" affixed to it. Labels are supplied on board the steamer.

Padlocks and leather straps should by all means be avoided, as the first are apt to be broken off in rough travelling, and the latter are liable to be cut. The Transit Administration refuses to be responsible for the *safe* carriage of carpet-bags, band-boxes, or such like. Valuable packages ought to be specially booked and paid for. All baggage ought to be shipped three days prior to the day of departure. Baggage may be insured if desired. No trunks, boxes, or portmanteaux allowed in the saloon or cabins.

The entire journey from Alexandria to Suez is performed in about forty hours, including a night's rest at Cairo, and a sufficient time for rest and refreshment at the Central Station between Cairo and Suez. When the railway across the desert is in full operation, this period will be shortened considerably.

Travelling costume ought to be light and loose. A Maud shawl is useful as a dressing-gown by day and a coverlet at night. A foraging-cap, or wide-awake, ought to be worn, having a white calico cover, and a curtain of the same material depending over the neck. This neck-preserver is of the utmost importance in hot climates. An umbrella, also covered with white calico, is essential as a parasol; and green or blue spectacles will be found of great advantage. A brown veil for the face while crossing the desert. A pouch or travelling-bag to sling over the shoulder is a most convenient appendage for cash, note-book, &c.

Carry nothing but sovereigns with you. *Half*-sovereigns should not be taken. And never pay the shop or hotel keepers with English gold, but get as much as you require exchanged at a money-changer's, and make yourself acquainted with the current rates of exchange. Be careful not to carry the small change of one country into another, as, generally speaking, in such cases it is valueless.

Take with you a pocket telescope and a good map of India. In regard to small conveniences,—such as needles, knives, scissors, &c., &c.,—we think that common sense is a sufficiently competent guide, and therefore content ourselves with the foregoing brief summary of information. More minute, though perhaps not less important, details will be found in the Hand-book already referred to.

A small library ought, of course, to be taken, in the selection of which the traveller will find an excellent assistant in Bradshaw's elaborate and comprehensive "Overland Guide to India." Among other volumes we may recommend Thornton's, Taylor & Mackenna's, and Elphinstone's Histories of India; Hamilton's East India Gazetteer, 2 vols.; Griffith's Journal Overland to India; Richardson's ditto; Bartlett's Overland Guide, and Bartlett's Nile Boat, &c.

Set your face as a flint against beggars,—give no backsheesh while you sojourn in the land of Egypt. Travellers who give none will be pestered; those who give it will be persecuted beyond endurance!